P9-CBU-083

DONATED BY

THE FRIENDS
OF
East Greenbush
Community
Library

Resisters and Rescuers—Standing Up Against the Holocaust

Titles in The Holocaust in History *Series*

—The Holocaust in History—

Resisters and Rescuers—Standing Up Against the Holocaust

Linda Jacobs Altman

Enslow Publishers, Inc.

40 Industrial Road   PO Box 38
Box 398   Aldershot
Berkeley Heights, NJ 07922 Hants GU12 6BP
USA   UK

http://www.enslow.com

Copyright © 2003 by Linda Jacobs Altman

All rights reserved.

No part of this book may be reproduced by any means without the written permission of the publisher.

Library of Congress Cataloging-in-Publication Data

Altman, Linda Jacobs, 1943-

    Resisters and rescuers : standing up against the Holocaust / Linda Jacobs Altman.
        p. cm. — (The Holocaust in history)
        Summary: Looks at how the Nazis took over Germany and different responses of people involved, particularly the many individuals and groups who fought back and helped to protect the victims of the Nazi regime.
        Includes bibliographical references and index.
        ISBN 0-7660-1994-2
        1. Holocaust, Jewish (1939-1945)—Juvenile literature. 2. World War, 1939-1945—Jewish resistance—Juvenile literature.
        3. Germany—History—1933-1945—Juvenile literature. [1. Holocaust, Jewish (1939-1945) 2. World War, 1939-1945—Jewish resistance. 3. Germany—History—1933-1945. 4. World War, 1939-1945—Jews—Rescue. 5. Righteous Gentiles in the Holocaust.] I. Title. II. Series.
        D804.34 .A498   2003
        940.53'183—dc21

                                        2002155860

Printed in the United States of America

10 9 8 7 6 5 4 3 2 1

To Our Readers: We have done our best to make sure all Internet Addresses in this book were active and appropriate when we went to press. However, the author and the publisher have no control over and assume no liability for the material available on those Internet sites or on other Web sites they may link to. Any comments or suggestions can be sent by e-mail to comments@enslow.com or to the address on the back cover.

Illustration Credits: Anne Frank Fonds-Basel/Anne Frank House-Amsterdam/Getty Images, p. 58; Enslow Publishers, Inc., pp. 8, 61; National Archives and Records Administration, pp. 2, 6, 10, 11, 12, 14, 16, 21, 35, 78, 80, 82, 84, 86, 88; USHMM, courtesy of Aveda Ayalon, p. 90; USHMM, courtesy of Beit Hannah Szenes, p. 43; USHMM, courtesy of Benjamin (Miedzyrzecki) Meed, p. 36; USHMM, courtesy of David Wherry, p. 63; USHMM courtesy of Frihedsmuseet, pp. 46, 56, 76; USHMM, courtesy of Hagstromer & Qviberg Fondkommission AB, p. 65; USHMM, courtesy of Hiroki Sugihara, pp. 60, 68, 70; USHMM, courtesy of the Israel Government Press Office, p. 51; USHMM, courtesy of Janine Klipstein Gimpelman Sokolov, pp. 5, 57; USHMM, courtesy of Julia Pirotte, pp. 1, 47; USHMM, courtesy of Leah Hammerstein Silverstein, p. 32; USHMM, courtesy of Leopold Page Photographic Collection, p. 72; USHMM, courtesy of Lena Kurtz Deutsch, p. 67; USHMM, courtesy of Library of Congress, p. 53; USHMM, courtesy of Main Commission for the Prosecution of the Crimes Against the Polish Nation, p. 26; USHMM, courtesy of Michael O'Hara, p. 17; USHMM, courtesy of Misha Lev, p. 41; USHMM, courtesy of Moshe Kaganovich, pp. 3, 48; USHMM, courtesy of National Archives, pp. 30, 38; USHMM, courtesy of Nederlands Instituut voor Oorlogsdocumentatie, p. 74; USHMM, courtesy of Sylvia Kramarski Kolski, p. 39; USHMM, courtesy of Yad Vashem Photo Archives, pp. 25, 28.

Cover Illustration: USHMM, courtesy of Yad Vashem Photo Archive

Contents

Adolf Hitler (standing in second row) salutes at a Nazi party rally in 1928. This was just the beginning of his rise to power.

Introduction
World War II and the Holocaust

On September 1, 1939, German troops invaded Poland. Two days later, Britain and France declared war on Germany. World War II had begun. Under Adolf Hitler and his National Socialist German Workers' Party, also called the Nazi party, Germany would soon conquer most of Europe.

Hitler planned to build a *Reich*, or empire, that would last for a thousand years. He believed that Northern Europeans, or Aryans as he called them, were a master race—a group of people superior to others.

Hitler falsely believed that some people were inferior, such as Jews, Gypsies, Poles, Russians, and people of color. These people would be given no rights in his Reich. Some would be exterminated, or killed. Others would be kept alive only so long as they served their Aryan masters. It was a dark and terrible vision that cost millions of lives.

In the early days of the war, Germany seemed unbeatable. One nation after another fell to the German *blitzkrieg*, or "lightning war." The Nazis conquered Poland in just twenty-six days. Denmark, Norway, Belgium, the Netherlands, and France fell in the spring of 1940.

By the end of 1940, the Germans had occupied most of Western Europe and made alliances with Italy and Japan. The Axis, as this alliance was called, soon conquered

By the end of 1940, the Germans had occupied most of Western Europe, including Poland, Luxembourg, Denmark, Norway, France, Belgium, and the Netherlands.

parts of Asia, Eastern Europe, and North Africa.

In 1941, the picture changed. In June, Germany invaded the Soviet Union, now called Russia. America entered the war on December 7, when Japan attacked the U.S. naval base in Pearl Harbor, Hawaii. The Germans soon found themselves fighting the British and the Americans in the West, and the Soviets in the East. They also devoted men and resources to exterminating Jews and other people the Nazis saw as inferior.

Even when the war turned against Germany, this slaughter did not stop. Trains that could have carried troops and supplies to the fighting fronts were used instead to transport victims to death camps. The killing continued until the last possible moment.

After Germany surrendered on May 7, 1945, survivors began telling what they had suffered. Pictures of starving prisoners, mass graves, and gas chambers disguised as showers appeared in newspapers and movie newsreels. People all over the world were horrified.

As survivors told their stories, the horror grew. New words came into the language. Old words took on new meanings. Holocaust came to represent mass murder on a scale that had never been seen before. Genocide

The Nazis quickly made their presence known throughout most of Europe. German police marched through Imst, Austria, in March 1938.

described the systematic killing of specific racial or ethnic groups.

These words are reminders of a grim truth—human beings can do terrible things to one another. This is why knowing about the Holocaust is so important. Knowledge is the best defense against the hatred that produced the Nazi racial state and caused the death of innocent millions.

Taking
a Stand

On January 30, 1933, Adolf Hitler became chancellor of Germany. In celebration, brown-uniformed Stormtroopers (also called the SA) marched through the streets of Berlin. Hitler watched from the open window of his new office as they passed below, their arms raised in the Nazi salute.

Hitler did not take power by war or revolution. He was appointed by President Paul von Hindenburg, on the advice of former Chancellor Franz von Papen.

Neither Papen nor Hindenburg liked Hitler. But times were hard in the Great Depression of the 1930s. During this time of economic hardship, thousands of people were out of work and were losing patience with the government. Hindenburg and Papen,

Paul von Hindenburg (left) greatly underestimated the power of Adolf Hitler (right).

with their aristocratic backgrounds and inherited wealth, could not reach these people. They believed Hitler could.

Papen believed that Hitler could be controlled. After all, he was just a poorly educated ex-corporal with a talent for speech making. He would be chancellor in name only. Others would hold the power. "In two months," said Papen, "we'll have pushed Hitler so far into a corner that he'll squeal."[1]

A Deadly Mistake

Papen was wrong. The day after taking office, Hitler used his new power to dissolve the Reichstag, the German Parliament, and call for new elections. He then set out to win those elections.

On the night of February 27, someone deliberately set fire to the Reichstag building. A Communist sympathizer named Marinus van der Lubbe was arrested for the crime.

Some historians believe that the Nazis themselves set the fire. Whether or not this was true, Hitler turned the situation to his own advantage. He convinced Hindenburg that the Reichstag fire was part of a vast Communist plot to take over Germany.

Hitler knew that the elderly president hated Communism. Hindenburg was an aristocrat—a privileged member of the upper

The fire at the Reichstag building broke out in twenty different places at the same time.

class. Communists wanted to do away with social classes altogether. Everyone would be equal and everything from steel mills to farmland and family homes would be run by the government.

When Hitler asked for emergency powers to "crush out this murderous pest with an iron fist," Hindenburg issued a presidential decree.[2] It suspended civil rights in Germany and gave Hitler the power to make laws on his own, without a vote of the Reichstag.

"Nazifying" German Life

In the election of March 5, 1933, the Nazis received 43.9 percent of the vote. By making alliances with other political parties, they put together a governing majority in the Reichstag.

Just seventeen days later, the first concentration camp began operations with two hundred political prisoners. The camp was called Dachau after a nearby town.

In time this name would take on a sinister meaning for anyone who opposed, or even criticized, the Nazi regime: "Keep quiet or you'll end up in Dachau," people told one another.[3]

The process of "Nazifying" Germany was both swift and brutal. It extended into every walk of life; from politics and science to art,

Germans give the Nazi salute as they burn banned books in 1933.

literature, and education. Schools became places for teaching Nazi ideas. Books from banned, or forbidden, writers were thrown onto giant bonfires. Paintings began to look more like propaganda posters than works of art. Nazi science followed the party line rather than the results of careful research.

Aryans, as Hitler called the northern Europeans, were promised an exciting future in the Reich. Jews, and other people the Nazis considered subhuman, were promised nothing.

Seeds of Resistance

The Nazis crushed resistance so unmercifully that only the most courageous would dare defy them. They used a large network of informers. This policy sowed distrust throughout German society. Workers informed on one another and on their bosses. Children informed on their teachers and even their parents. No one was safe unless he or she followed the Nazi line.

The Nazis lost no time in teaching children how to behave and in what to believe. Here, a portrait of Adolf Hitler overlooks a geography lesson in an all-boy class in Nazi Germany.

Young people learned the rules quickly. Some were glad to use this new power. Years after the war, Ilse McKee remembered how teachers at her grammar school came to fear their students:

> Most of [the teachers] had been doubtful about Hitler, but unless they wanted to lose their jobs they had to . . . turn in his direction. . . . Some of the children in each class would not hesitate to act as informers. . . . Many were dismissed and it was dangerous to act as anything but a [Nazi].[4]

McKee's father despised the Nazis, but he joined the party anyway. He enrolled her in the League of German Girls, because that is what the Party expected—and demanded. He tried to keep out of trouble without giving in totally to the Nazis.

Some Germans went further than this silent disapproval. For example, Ilse-Margret Vogel was a young woman living and working in Berlin when Hitler came to power. She and her friends hated him. "We cannot boast great deeds," wrote Vogel. "We did not [kill] or physically harm any Nazis, but we did frequently risk our lives . . . by helping people . . . who were being pursued and persecuted."[5]

Vogel's group stopped short of open opposition. They did not make anti-Nazi speeches or arm themselves to fight. They helped people who were in trouble while going about their regular lives. So did many other

Germans who secretly opposed Hitler and resented the loss of personal freedom.

Resistance and Religion

Some clergymen considered resistance to Nazism a moral duty. The Church preached peace; the Nazis made war. The Church taught compassion for all members of society; the Nazis wanted to kill many of them. In a Nazi world, only the strong would survive.

Adolf Hitler was raised in the Christian religion. However, he did not practice Christianity's principles of love and forgiveness. He considered them to be signs of weakness.

The Nazis used religion like they used everything else—as a tool for controlling the masses. If that tool were to cause a problem, it would be crushed.

A group calling itself the "German Christians" tried to combine Christianity with Nazism. They wanted to limit membership in German churches to people of Aryan blood. By this racial test, thousands of lifelong Christians could suddenly be classified as Jews. In a Nazified society, that classification could be a death sentence.

Reverend Martin Niemoeller and Reverend Deidrich Bonhoeffer formed the Confessing Church to oppose the German Christians. Christians were Christians, they said, regardless of background. To believe otherwise was to oppose Biblical teaching.

The Confessing Church did not openly defy all of Nazi Jewish policy. It concentrated on protecting Christians of Jewish background, including converts and people with Jewish ancestors.

Undoubtedly, the leaders knew they were taking a risk, even with this limited action. It was a risk they felt they had to take. Niemoeller summed up the hard truth in words that became famous:

> First they came for the Communists, but I was not a Communist so I did not speak out. Then they came for the Socialists and Trade Unionists, but I was neither, so I did not speak out. Then they came for the Jews, but I was not a Jew so I did not speak out. And when they came for me, there was no one left to speak out for me.[6]

Speaking out took courage, even for people in positions of leadership. Such was Hitler's power that neither fame, wealth, nor social position could protect his enemies. Martin Niemoeller spent most of the war years in a series of concentration camps. Deidrich Bonhoeffer, who later became involved in the military plot to assassinate Hitler, was hanged for treason after the attempt failed.

The White Rose

Hans and Sophie Scholl were teenagers when the Nazis came to power. Both became enthusiastic members of the Hitler Youth. Like others in their group, the Scholls believed that Adolf Hitler would lead Germany out of its troubles.

Then the Nazis began to tighten their grip on the people. Mental patients and other "defective" people were killed by the thousands in isolated hospitals. Jews were stripped of their rights and property simply

Hans and Sophie Scholl were active in the Hitler Youth before they turned against the Nazis. Here, members of the group honor the Hour of Commemoration in Tomaszow, Poland, on May 11, 1941.

because they were Jews. The Scholls' father, Robert, was jailed because an informer overheard him call Hitler "God's scourge on mankind."[7]

After their father's imprisonment, Hans and Sophie turned against Nazism. Their sister Inge, who survived the war, later compared their new awareness to "a feeling of living in a house once beautiful and clean but in whose cellars behind locked doors frightful, evil, and fearsome things were happening."[8]

As students at the University of Munich, Hans and Sophie began discussing politics with like-minded friends. In time, all agreed that endless discussions were not enough. They had to do something.

Under the name "White Rose," the Scholls and their friends wrote and distributed a series of anti-Nazi leaflets. These leaflets called all Germans of goodwill to passive resistance.

Passive resistance meant many things, from not flying the Nazi flag or joining the Nazi Party to secretly helping Jews and other victims. It meant disrupting public gatherings, sabotaging factories, doing anything to slow the war effort without physically hurting anyone.

In February, 1943, Hans and Sophie Scholl were caught distributing leaflets. Another

White Rose leader, Christoph Probst, was arrested later. After a hasty unfair trial, all three were executed. Three other leaders later paid with their lives for opposing the Führer (another name for Hitler, literally meaning "leader.")

The students who gave their lives did not topple Hitler's Reich. They did not even shorten the war. What they did do was become examples of courage in the face of unbeatable odds. In World War II Germany, that was an important achievement.

The Edelweiss Pirates

Another anti-Nazi youth movement came to be known by the colorful name of "Edelweiss Pirates." (Edelweiss is a European flowering herb.) Many of these teenagers were not especially interested in moral or political issues. Their resistance was cultural.

The Edelweiss Pirates did not want to march through life in lockstep with the Hitler Youth. They dressed oddly, often in leather shorts, checkered shirts, and neck scarves. They listened to the "wrong" music, wrote protest poems, and liked nothing better than picking fights with Hitler Youth.

Some Pirates did engage in serious anti-Nazi activity. For example, one group plotted to blow up Gestapo headquarters in the city of Cologne. The Gestapo was the feared secret police of Nazi Germany. Under the leadership of twenty-four-year-old Hans Steinbrück, the Pirates stockpiled weapons and ammunition for the attack.

Steinbrück was older than most Pirates, but otherwise typical. He was a former Hitler Youth member who ran afoul of the Gestapo and was briefly imprisoned. The experience left him bitter and vengeful.

Steinbrück and his young collaborators never got the chance to carry out their plan. The Gestapo sniffed out the plot and arrested them. Steinbrück and several others were executed as traitors to the Reich.

Like the White Rose and other resisters, the Edelweiss Pirates achieved something even in failure. They became part of the story of German resistance to Adolf Hitler and his evil empire.

The Resistance Fighters

Adolf Hitler once said that "people more easily fall victim to a big lie than to a little one."[1] The Nazis took this to heart. They used lying as a means of controlling their victims.

Jews bound for extermination centers were told they were going to work camps. At the killing centers, a few Jews from each transport would be selected to live for a time as slave laborers. The rest were sent straight to gas chambers that were disguised as shower rooms.

Attendants handed out soap and washcloths as the victims filed inside. By the time these people realized what was happening to them, it was too late. Poisonous gas had begun to seep into the tightly locked room.

This is a door to a gas chamber that the Nazis used at Auschwitz concentration camp. The note in German on the door reads: "Harmful gas! Entering endangers your life." The Jews who died in these gas chambers did not get such a warning.

Hope for Survival

Not all Jews were fooled, but they were unarmed and vastly outnumbered. Direct attack on German forces would have been suicidal and senseless.

Martyrdom, or dying for a cause, appears often in Jewish history, But senseless death is an affront to everything Jews hold dear. Jews regard life as a precious thing. So long as there is even a hint of hope, they will do whatever seems most likely to preserve it. The Nazis knew how to make this work to their advantage.

One tactic was to hold the entire Jewish community responsible for the acts of any member. For example, a group of twenty-one young Jews slipped out of the ghetto in Vilna, Lithuania. They planned to join a band of partisans, or freedom fighters.

Along the way, they were ambushed by a German patrol. When the fighting was over, nine Jews lay dead in the road. The Nazis tracked down families, friends, and neighbors of the dead men and executed them as well. When that was done, they posted a notice in the ghetto: "The family of everyone who escapes . . . will be executed. If the family cannot be found, the escapees' roommates will be executed; if these cannot be found, all the tenants of his building will be executed."[2]

Some Jews joined partisan groups and fought against the Nazis. This is a group from the Soviet Molotova brigade, which included several Jewish units.

Facing a Terrible Truth

As the situation in the ghettos worsened, many Jews lost hope. They gave up trying to stay alive. For these people, death came quickly. Some would deliberately run to the ghetto border, inviting the guards to shoot. Others quietly starved. But some turned to fight, determined that Jewish lives would cost the Nazis dearly.

In Vilna, an intense young poet named Abba Kovner called the ghetto to resistance. There was no safe haven for Jews, he said; no chance for rescue. "Perhaps [some] Jews will be saved; but for our people as a whole . . . there is no chance. Is there any way out? Yes. Revolt and armed self-defense. This is the only way which promises any dignity for our people."[3]

In Warsaw, Poland, massive deportations from the ghetto brought other Jews to the same conclusion. Beginning on July 22, 1942, and continuing into September, the Nazis deported three hundred thousand Jews.

The Jews left the ghetto in long trains of cattle cars. No one knew just where they were going, but most of them would never be heard from again.

On July 28, just one week after the deportations began, a group of young Jews formed the Jewish fighting organization, or ZOB after its Polish initials. They had no weapons, no military training, and no master strategy for defending the ghetto.

What they did have was a desire to face the truth and rouse the ghetto to action. Those trains were not headed for work camps or even prison camps, they said. They were carrying their fellow Jews to extermination centers.

Many people refused to believe that even the Nazis could kill so many in cold blood. The very idea was not only monstrous; it did not make sense.

The SS (right) operated the ghettos and camps. They quickly became feared in the Warsaw ghetto.

The Germans had their hands full fighting the British, Americans, and Russians. They needed more workers for their factories and farms. Why would they kill people whose labor could be used in the war effort?

The resistance leaders could not answer this question. But neither could they ignore the facts before them. They began to gather weapons, going outside the ghetto to beg, buy, or steal them. Sooner or later, the Germans would come in force to wipe out the ghetto. The resisters meant to be ready when that happened.

The First Skirmish

On January 18, 1943, a shock ran through the ghetto. The Germans had begun another round of deportations. People who had said it would not happen again saw how wrong they were. Resistance fighters feared that this would be the ghetto's final hour.

One teacher and historian wrote about the January deportations in a secret diary: "Our mood is very gloomy and depressed. News . . . indicates that the Germans intend to finish off the Jews completely. They will not leave a single Jew alive. . . . We fear that [this] . . . will be the last for all of us."[4]

The resistance fighters were not ready for a major battle. The best they could do was form small groups to act by themselves. For example, ghetto organizer Mordecai Anielewicz hand-picked a dozen armed fighters to slip into the lines of people waiting to be deported.

At a signal, each fighter attacked the nearest German guard. The action took the soldiers by surprise. Before they could return fire, hundreds of Jews scattered and ran for cover.

The battle in the streets did not last long. The Germans made quick work of the fighters. Still, the psychological effect of this action was powerful. The Jews began thinking of

Mordecai Anielewicz (standing, on right) poses with other members of the Hashomer Hatzair Socialist Zionist youth movement in 1938. In November 1942, he became commander of the ZOB and led the Warsaw ghetto uprising.

themselves as fighters rather than simply victims. Many no longer thought that obedience to the Germans offered the best chance of survival.

The Germans learned from these events. They began to realize that destroying the ghetto might not be as easy as they had thought. When the time came, they would have to make a show of force.

Last Stand in Warsaw

On April 19, 1943, at four o'clock in the morning, the Germans marched on the ghetto. They had tanks, cannons, and armored cars. The soldiers carried automatic machine guns.

Against this overwhelming force, the resistance fighters went into action. This time, they were not caught without a plan. Mordecai Anielewicz, who had disrupted the deportations in January, had fighting units stationed all around the ghetto. He commanded them from a bunker at 18 Mila Street.

The Jewish fighters were both brave and clever. They harried the Germans from rooftops and alleyways, using mostly handguns and homemade bombs. They hid in bunkers and moved through ancient tunnels beneath the streets.

The Jews knew they could not win. They knew that most of them would die in the fighting. They abandoned hope and fought as people with nothing left to lose. This very hopelessness made them dangerous enemies.

The Germans were stunned. They had marched into the ghetto expecting a quick victory. Instead, they faced fierce attacks from an enemy that struck from nowhere and disappeared.

Impatient Killers

By the fourth day, SS Reichführer Heinrich Himmler was outraged. To him, it was unthinkable that a poorly armed group of racial inferiors could hold the German army at bay.

Himmler personally contacted General Jürgen Stroop, commander of German troops in the ghetto. He ordered the general to "complete the combing out of the Warsaw Ghetto with the greatest severity and relentless tenacity."[5]

Because ordinary battle tactics did not work in the ghetto, Stroop had to find another way. He ordered his men "to destroy the entire Jewish residential area by setting every block on fire."[6]

When the fires began, Vladka Meed was outside the ghetto. She had been posing as a gentile in order to send guns, ammunition, and information to the resistance forces. Now

Heinrich Himmler (left with glasses) was a top Nazi leader. Here, he is seen inspecting a prisoner-of-war camp in Russia.

she stood by an upstairs window, watching the ghetto burn:

> The crackling of dry woodwork, the occasional collapse of a weakened floor were the only sounds heard in the eerie stillness that had settled over [the ghetto] while the blazing buildings turned night into day. All night long I stood at the window . . . the heat scorching my face, the smoke burning my eyes, and watched the flames consume the ghetto.[7]

Vladka Meed was very important to the Jewish underground in Warsaw. It was while in this service that she met her husband, Ben Meed. He, too, soon joined the underground, where he became very accomplished at constructing hiding places for Jews.

The End of the Ghettos

In this nightmare world of smoke and flame, the Jews continued to fight. They continued even after the Nazis destroyed the command bunker and killed Mordecai Anielewicz. Only after a month could Stroop tell Himmler that the Warsaw Ghetto had ceased to exist.

No one knows exactly how many Jews died in the uprising. Stroop reported that "the continuous and untiring work of all involved" resulted in "catching a total of 56,065 Jews whose extermination can be proved."[8]

A few hundred Jews managed to escape the burning ghetto. Some of them made their way to the "Polish side" of Warsaw and blended in with the non-Jewish population. Others headed out of the city, to the forests and farmlands of the countryside. Many of these Jews joined or formed partisan groups to continue the fight against the Nazis.

The Warsaw Jews were not the only ghetto inhabitants to revolt against the Nazis. In 1943 alone, there were also uprisings in Bedzin, Sosnowiec, Bialystok, and Vilna. In each case, Jews rose up when it became clear that their ghettos were to be destroyed. Many of the fighters were teenagers. Like their comrades in Warsaw, these desperate young

Jürgen Stroop (second from left in foreground) watches buildings in the Warsaw ghetto burn. Stroop later documented the destruction of the Warsaw ghettos in words and pictures for his Nazi superiors.

people did not expect to win. They expected only to die with dignity.

They had no way of knowing that the destruction of each ghetto was part of a larger scheme. In June 1943, Heinrich Himmler decided that the ghettos had outlived their usefulness. On June 8, he ordered the destruction of all ghettos in Poland. On June 21, he gave the same order for ghettos in the German-occupied areas of the Soviet Union.

In each case, the Germans came in force. They killed as many people as possible, then

This memorial by Nathan Rapaport in Warsaw honors those who took part in the ghetto uprising.

rounded up the survivors and sent most of them to extermination centers.

Uprisings in the Camps

In the extermination centers, life was built around death. Most victims went straight from the trains to the gas chambers. The few kept alive to work knew full well what would happen to them when the work was done.

They saw the dead bodies in the "showers." They knew that obedience would not save their lives. Their only chance lay in escape.

The camp uprisings occurred at a time when Germany was barely able to deal with them. By the summer of 1943, the Germans had lost North Africa and Sicily. Their alliance with Italy fell apart after Italian dictator Benito Mussolini was removed from power on July 25, 1943.

Just a week later, the inmates of the Treblinka death camp revolted. Armed with picks, shovels, and a few stolen weapons they attacked the SS men who ran the camp. They set fires in part of the camp and stormed the barbed wire fences while the guards were busy dealing with the blaze. Only two hundred people got out of the camp. Half of them were later recaptured and executed.

The prisoners of Sobibor revolted on October 14, after weeks of preparation. Before making their stand, they cut phone and electricity lines into the camp and sabotaged all motor vehicles. Just before evening roll call, they quietly killed as many SS guards as possible and took their rifles.

When the prisoners were standing at roll call, one of the guards saw the body of an SS man and raised the alarm. The prisoners broke for the gates and the forest beyond.

There were six hundred prisoners in the camp that day. Three hundred of them escaped. They split into small groups and

Pictured are some of the few survivors of the Sobibor death-camp uprising.

headed off in different directions. About one hundred fifty were never recaptured. However, roughly one hundred of them were later killed fighting Germans or while in hiding. As a result, only about fifty of those participating in the uprising survived the war.

Hannah Szenes—Hero From the Homeland

Unlike Jewish freedom fighters in Europe, Hannah Szenes was not caught up in the Nazi extermination machine. When the war broke out in 1939, she was safe in Palestine (present-day Israel). Her life on a kibbutz, or communal farming settlement, was satisfying and full.

Szenes gave up this safety to help Jews in her native Hungary. She became part of a daring mission into the heart of Nazi-controlled Europe. Szenes was one of thirty-three young Jews who went through intensive training with the British Army.

On the night of March 13, 1944, these young people parachuted into Yugoslavia. They linked up with non-Jewish partisans to rescue downed pilots, help local partisans, and smuggle Jews to safety. The work started in Yugoslavia because Hungarian Jews were not under immediate threat.

Hannah Szenes sits in her garden in Budapest, Hungary, in the mid 1930s.

Hungary was an ally of Germany, so it was not occupied by German troops. So far, Hungarian authorities had refused to turn their Jewish citizens over to the Nazis. That was about to change.

Just six days after Szenes arrived in Yugoslavia, German troops marched into Hungary. They dissolved the government and installed a puppet regime that would follow their orders.

Hannah Szenes knew what that meant for Jews. The horror that had happened in the rest of Eastern Europe now began in Hungary. First there were new anti-Jewish laws, then roundups and the formation of ghettos. Finally, the deportations began. Jews were sent out of Hungary by the trainload. Many of them went to Auschwitz-Birkenau, where most were immediately gassed.

Hannah Szenes was determined to make her way into Hungary and do what she could to help. She made her way across the Yugoslavian border on June 7. The next day she was captured by a German patrol.

In German custody, she was beaten, tortured, and put through a sham trial. On November 7, 1944, twenty-three-year-old Hannah Szenes was executed by a firing squad. According to witnesses, she refused a blindfold.

Today, Hannah Szenes is considered a hero. Every schoolchild in Israel is taught her name and her story. Like other Jewish fighters, Hannah Szenes's actions cannot be judged by ordinary standards. Neither the parachutists, the ghetto fighters, nor the forest partisans defeated their enemies or even won an important battle.

What they did do was act with uncommon courage against impossible odds. In the process, they served notice that the Germans were not as all-powerful as Hitler wanted them to be.

An Uncertain Freedom

Jewish resistance during World War II was not limited to the ghettos and camps. Some Jews managed to escape Nazi control. Many joined partisan groups to fight behind enemy lines. Others survived by pretending to be gentiles, or non-Jews. Still others went into hiding, leading secret lives as they waited out the war.

These people paid a high price for their uncertain freedom. Each lived looking over his or her shoulder, suspicious of every stranger. They had to be ready at all times to run, fight, or talk themselves out of a tight spot. It was not a way of life for the faint-hearted.

The Jewish Partisans

There were Jewish partisan groups in both Eastern and Western Europe. Most western

These Jewish partisans are in the middle of an insurrection in the south of France in August 1944.

activity took place in France, where a group known as the "Jewish Army" operated. In addition to fighting Germans, this partisan group was deeply involved in saving Jews. Members smuggled money into the country for relief efforts and smuggled people out to safety in neutral Spain.

In Eastern Europe, many Jews who escaped the Germans lived as partisans in the deep, ancient forests of the region. They raided enemy positions, sabotaged supply lines, and disrupted communications. Like the units in France, some of them also

Members of Tuvia Bielski's partisan group took a break from guard duty at an airstrip in Naliboki Forest in Belarus to pose for this portrait. Tuvia Bielski himself is not in the picture.

provided a haven for Jews escaping German control.

For example, Tuvia Bielski and his two brothers formed a partisan unit in the Naliboki Forest of Lithuania. From the beginning in 1941, they took in refugees who were too old, too young, or too sick for fighting. By 1943, their camp was like a small village, with workshops of various kinds.

Some argued that it was a mistake to take in so many people who could not fight. Tuvia Bielski did not agree. He believed that there was strength in numbers. The young, fit members of the colony did the fighting. The rest supported them.

Non-fighters repaired weapons, made clothing, cooked meals, and generally helped in any way possible. About ten thousand Jews survived the war in the partisan camps.[1]

Carrying on the Fight

As the ghettos were liquidated, or done away with, more people escaped to the forests. In Vilna, Lithuania, resistance leader Abba Kovner and his people got out just in time. They went through the sewers under the city, feeling their way through the cold stone tunnels.

Abba Kovner was an unlikely warrior. Before the Nazis came, he was a gentle young poet. The senseless brutality of the Nazis turned him into a hardened fighter. When it came to fighting Nazis, no sacrifice was too great for Kovner.

Unlike partisan leaders such as Tuvia Bielski, he would not allow people who could not fight to live with his partisans. Those who joined him left their families behind.

In making this harsh demand, Kovner did not ask for anything he would not do himself. With great pain, he left his own mother in the ghetto.

Only fighters could make good this daring escape, he told her. Others would surely not survive the journey, let alone the hard life that awaited them in the forest.

The Avengers

Rudniki Forest was combed through with partisan camps when Abba Kovner and his people arrived. They linked up with an underground led by escaped Soviet prisoners of war. According to some estimates, there may have been as many as thirty thousand partisans in the forest.[2]

Abba Kovner and other Jews received a harsh reception. Many of the Russian and Lithuanian partisans were strongly anti-Semitic. Some refused to work with Jews. Some even attacked them.

Kovner was determined that this would not stop him. His unit, code-named "The Avengers," had come to fight Germans and fight them they would. Not even lack of weapons and supplies could stop them.

When the Avengers had no ammunition, they sabotaged unguarded equipment. For example, they learned to dig up small sections of railroad tracks and disguise the break so the trainmen would not notice until it was

On May 4, 1961, Abba Kovner (pictured) testified at the trial of Adolf Eichmann, who headed the Nazi department in charge of the Final Solution. Eichmann was found guilty and executed on May 31, 1962.

too late to stop. They wrecked many supply trains in this way, without using a single bullet, bomb, or grenade.

Posing as Gentiles

Living as outlaws in swampy forests was not for everyone. Some Jews managed to hide in plain sight, by posing as gentiles. This was not an easy thing to do. It required a new name, forged identity papers, and a certain ability to play a part.

People who did not "look Jewish" had the best chance of success. According to Nazi stereotypes, Jews were short, dark people with prominent noses. Blond and blue-eyed Jews could pass for gentiles.

Physical appearance alone was not enough. Language and behavior also played a part. A Jew masquerading as a gentile could not speak with a Yiddish accent. Yiddish was the language of East European Jews. Few, if any, gentiles spoke or understood it.

Also, familiarity with Christian and other non-Jewish customs could sometimes be necessary. For example, when Polish Christians saw a funeral procession going by, they would genuflect, or bend the knee, and make the sign of the cross. Jews who were posing as gentiles quickly learned to do the same.

Deutsche Jugend

Jüdische Jugend

14jähriger deutscher Junge · 14jähriger deutscher Junge · 14jähriger Judenjunge · 13jähriger Judenjunge

13jähriges deutsches Mädchen · 8jähriges deutsches Mädchen · 8jähriges Judenmädchen · 14jähriges Judenmädchen

7jähriger deutscher Junge · 7jähriger Judenjunge

Aus dem Gesicht spricht die Seele der Rasse

This chart was meant to be an aid in determining whether a child was a Jew or a gentile. It appeared in a textbook by Alfred Vogel, published in 1938.

Simon and Cyla Wiesenthal are good examples, both of Jews who could "pass" and those who could not. Simon Wiesenthal "looked Jewish," which is to say his appearance fit the Nazi stereotype. He spoke with a pronounced Yiddish accent. His wife Cyla was a blue-eyed blond who spoke Polish with no accent at all.

With the help of underground contacts, Cyla was able to get false papers with a Polish name: Irena Kowalska. She lived in Warsaw and worked in a radio factory. Her husband went through a series of work camps and concentration camps. Both survived and were reunited after the war.

The Wanderers

Some Jews stayed free by moving from place to place, working on small family farms for food and perhaps a sleeping mat in the barn. Alicia Jurman started doing this when she was only thirteen years old. She was fair-skinned and pretty, with a rosy, country-girl glow that people found appealing.

She made up her gentile identity as she went along, changing it to suit the circumstances. In the areas she covered, she could run into Poles or Ukrainians. Since the two peoples generally hated each other, the choice was a matter of some importance:

I tried to imitate the free, swaying walk of the village girls. . . . I had to be careful approaching the farmers to ask for work; what if I addressed one in Ukranian and he turned out to be Polish? He would certainly turn me away and then I wold have lost the chance to work and get a piece of bread. . . . On the other hand, If I spoke Polish to a Ukranian, something even worse could happen—the man might come after me with his shovel. So the first moment that I approached the farmers was always crucial. On my way across the field I always tried to swing close to the other workers and listen to [them] to find out which language to use.[3]

Alicia Jurman learned the lessons of survival well. She could recognize when to stay, when to go, and when to hide until danger had passed.

Hiding Places

Hiding places were important survival tools for many Jews. People found places in cellars, behind false walls, beneath loose floorboards. They would go about their usual lives until danger threatened, then slip into their hideaways until it passed. People who could hide well enough for long enough had a chance to survive.

Some people actually lived in hiding. They could not do this without help. Someone had to supply them with food and other necessities. This was dangerous work.

During the Holocaust, hiding was very important to Jews for survival. Here, a Jewish man happily comes out of hiding once the Danish fishing boat he is on enters Swedish waters. Sweden remained neutral during World War II, and many escaped Jews found refuge there.

In German-occupied Europe, the penalty for hiding Jews was imprisonment or death.

For adults, long-term hiding was often not practical. Hiding children was more common. A number of Jewish families placed their children with Christians who would hide them.

Eleven-year-old Renee Roth and her two younger sisters survived the war in a Catholic convent. The nuns taught the girls how to behave like Catholics when necessary and also kept them out of sight when trouble threatened.

Years later, Renee Roth wrote about her experiences and the women who had saved her: "How I admired the nuns' selflessness and brave spirit—their risking their lives by taking us in, their scouring the countryside for food in those times of severe rationing."[4]

The best-known true story of a life in hiding is that of Anne Frank. She was thirteen years old when the Germans invaded

Nuns often hid Jewish children. Here, Sister Huberte poses with a group of children at the Soeurs de Sainte Marie convent near Braine-l'Alleud, Belgium. Many of those pictured are Jewish children in hiding.

Anne Frank was one of the many Jewish children who had to go into hiding.

Holland and destroyed the life she and her family had known. Anne's father Otto set up a walled-off apartment at the back of a factory he owned.

On July 6, 1942, the Franks and several other Jews entered hiding in this "secret annex" as they called it. They lived there for more than two years, while Anne wrote her famous diary. In August, 1944, an unknown informer betrayed the Franks to the Germans. The SS raided the secret annex and sent all of its residents to concentration camps. Anne and her older sister Margot died at the Bergen-Belsen camp in March 1945. An added note of tragedy in Anne's death is that Bergen-Belsen was liberated on April 15, a few short weeks after she died.

Otto Frank was the only person from the secret annex to survive the war. He saw to it that his daughter's diary was published. For him, it was a labor of love. For the world, the diary became a symbol of the Holocaust.

There are no records to show exactly how many Jews survived because they were able to evade the Nazis. There are only stories of individuals struggling against an inhuman system. Regardless of the outcome in any particular case, that struggle itself was an act of courage.

To Save
a People

At the Yad Vashem Holocaust museum in Israel, there is a broad walkway lined with carob trees; more than six hundred of them. This is the Avenue of the Righteous. Each tree bears a plaque with the name of a gentile who risked his or her life to save Jews from the Holocaust. These trees and these names have become a symbol of human decency in the midst of unthinkable evil.

The six hundred honored here are only a small representation of the thousands of people that Yad Vashem has called Righteous Among the Nations. As of January 1, 2003, 19,706 have been so honored. They came from different nations and different walks of life. Some saved hundreds, or even thousands. Others saved a few.

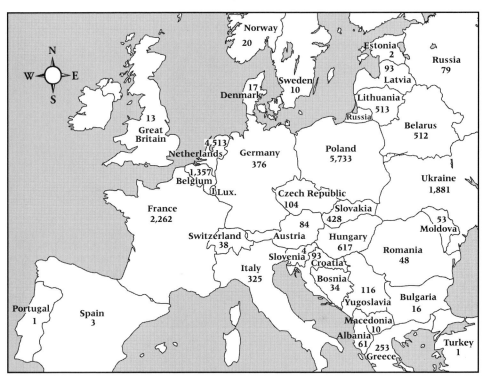

Each European country's number of Righteous Among the Nations is shown above. (Note on Denmark's figure: The Danish Underground asked that all its members be listed as one group, not individually; Otherwise, the country of Denmark's figure would have been much larger.)

In the Jewish tradition, all are worthy of honor. The Jewish philosopher Maimonides, who lived in the twelfth century, once said that when someone saves one human life, it is as if that person had saved the entire world.

Responding to Need

Stories of rescuers offer one of the few bright spots in the long and terrible history of the Holocaust. Rescuers did not consider themselves special. When asked about their work, most would say they simply saw a need and filled it.

"I am not a hero," said Miep Gies, one of the people who cared for Anne Frank's family in hiding. "I stand at the end of a long, long line of good Dutch people who did what I did or more—much more—during those dark and terrible times. . . ."[1]

For all her work, Gies was not able to save the Frank family. An unknown informer took that out of her hands. The Gestapo was skilled at getting ordinary people to betray coworkers, neighbors, and even friends. They rewarded informers with small cash payments or luxuries such as liquor, sugar, and cigarettes.

Rescuers, on the other hand, had nothing to gain and everything to lose. Many were

A concentration camp was one fate that awaited a rescuer if he or she was caught. Here, Jewish survivors of the Buchenwald camp lie in their bunks, suffering from malnutrition and disease.

sent to concentration camps, where they starved, slaved, and often died. Many were executed. The Germans were especially quick to execute Poles and Russians, whom they considered racially inferior.

Historians and other scholars have long tried to understand rescuers. What did people who helped have in common with one another? That is not an easy question to answer. Helpers came from different social backgrounds and stations in life. Some were rich and some were poor. Some were educated and some were not.

Most did not plan to get into rescue work. It just happened. They saw someone in need and helped out as best they could. They faced personal danger because they believed it was the right thing to do.

Raoul Wallenberg—The Gift of Life

Raoul Wallenberg came from a wealthy and distinguished Swedish banking family. His grandfather tried to interest him in a career in finance, but Raoul had other ideas.

"I am not made to be a banker," he once wrote to his grandfather. ". . . I think that my talents lie elsewhere. I want to do something more positive than sit behind a desk all day saying no to people."[2]

Raoul Wallenberg is seen here in a passport photo.

Wallenberg found his calling in Hungary in 1944. Although the war was clearly lost, the Nazis had begun their destruction of the Hungarian Jewry. With the help of United States Ambassador Herschel V. Johnson, Wallenberg became a diplomat with the Swedish embassy in Budapest. He was also given money to finance a Jewish rescue operation.

He did not hesitate to use the money to bribe German and Hungarian bureaucrats. In this way, he was able to get some Jews to safety, but the process was far too slow. The Germans were deporting Jews by the thousands. Wallenberg was only able to save them by the hundreds. Something had to be done.

After much consideration, Wallenberg created a new kind of official document—the Schutzpass. It was a combination passport and immigration certificate. It said that the bearer was immigrating to Sweden and therefore was protected by the Swedish government.

With the war going against them, the Nazis were not eager to offend neutral Sweden. The Schutzpasses worked! The Swedish government authorized Wallenberg to hand out forty-five hundred of these documents. Wallenberg ignored this limit.

He handed out many thousands. He would go to the deportation trains and give

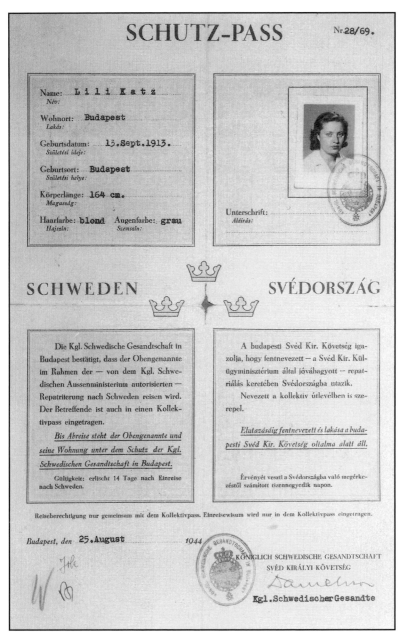

SCHUTZ-PASS

Nr. 28/69.

Name: **Lili Katz**
Név:

Wohnort: **Budapest**
Lakás:

Geburtsdatum: **13.Sept.1913.**
Születési ideje:

Geburtsort: **Budapest**
Születési helye:

Körperlänge: **164 cm.**
Magasság:

Haarfarbe: **blond** Augenfarbe: **grau**
Hajszín: *Szemszín:*

Unterschrift:
Aláírás:

SCHWEDEN ✦ SVÉDORSZÁG

Die Kgl. Schwedische Gesandtschaft in Budapest bestätigt, dass der Obengenannte im Rahmen der — von dem Kgl. Schwedischen Aussenministerium autorisierten — Repatriierung nach Schweden reisen wird. Der Betreffende ist auch in einen Kollektivpass eingetragen.

Bis Abreise steht der Obengenannte und seine Wohnung unter dem Schutz der Kgl. Schwedischen Gesandtschaft in Budapest.

Gültigkeit: erlischt 14 Tage nach Einreise nach Schweden.

A budapesti Svéd Kir. Követség igazolja, hogy fentnevezett — a Svéd Kir. Külügyminisztérium által jóváhagyott — repatriálás keretében Svédországba utazik.

Nevezett a kollektiv útlevélben is szerepel.

Elutazásáig fentnevezett és lakása a budapesti Svéd Kir. Követség oltalma alatt áll.

Érvényét veszti a Svédországba való megérkezéstől számított tizennegyedik napon.

Reiseberechtigung nur gemeinsam mit dem Kollektivpass. Einreisevisum wird nur in dem Kollektivpass eingetragen.

Budapest, den **25.August** 1944

KÖNIGLICH SCHWEDISCHE GESANDTSCHAFT
SVÉD KIRÁLYI KÖVETSÉG

Kgl.Schwedischer Gesandte

This Schutzpass was issued to Lili Katz. Raoul Wallenberg has initialed the bottom-left corner of the document.

out Schutzpasses. Then he would race ahead to the next stop and angrily accuse the SS of deporting Swedish citizens. With help from other neutral governments, Wallenberg set up safe houses for the Jews he rescued.

Raoul Wallenberg saved at least twenty thousand Hungarian Jews from certain death. Wallenberg himself was arrested by the Soviets after the war. He died in their custody, apparently in 1947.

Chiune Sugihara—The Right Thing to Do

Like Raoul Wallenberg, Chiune Sugihara used his position as a diplomat to save Jewish

Chiune Sugihara sits at his desk in China in the 1930s.

lives. Sugihara represented Japan in the small Eastern European nation of Lithuania.

After Nazi Germany invaded Poland in September 1939, many Polish Jews fled to Lithuania. These people desperately needed a safe haven. Their best chance lay eastward toward Japan, but they could not cross international borders without visas, or travel permits.

In July 1940, a great crowd of Polish Jews went to the Japanese Consulate in Kaunas, Lithuania. They had come to ask Chiune Sugihara for help. Sugihara sympathized with their plight. He knew that if the Nazis got hold of these people, most of them would die.

However it would be tough to get his government to agree because Germany and Japan were allies in World War II. He contacted his superiors in Tokyo, asking permission to issue the visas. They turned him down. That should have ended the matter, but Chiune Sugihara could not let go. He asked again, and yet again. Still the answer was no, and still the refugees waited outside, their faces haggard yet hopeful.

Sugihara knew that defying orders could cost him his career in the diplomatic service. He also knew he was going to issue those visas. "I may have to disobey my government, but if I [didn't] I would be disobeying God," he said.[3]

From July 31 to August 28, 1940, Chiune Sugihara and his wife Yukiko worked feverishly, issuing the life-saving documents. Hundreds of visas became thousands. The Sugiharas did not quit until they were forced to close the consulate. Even then, Sugihara continued issuing visas. He handed out dozens from the window of the train that would take him and his family to an uncertain future.

The Sugihara family sits in the living room of their home in Kaunas, Lithuania, in September 1939. Seated from left to right: Setsuko Kikuchi (Yukiko's sister) and Chiune, Chiaki, Hiroki, and Yukiko Sugihara.

About six thousand Jewish refugees made their way to Japan on the Sugihara visas. Later, most of them went on to Shanghai, China. There, they passed the war in safety.

After the war ended in 1945, Chiune Sugihara was forced to resign from the Japanese diplomatic service. He never talked about his heroism. The story came out through survivors who owed their lives to him. In 1985, he was honored with a carob tree on the Avenue of the Righteous at Yad Vashem. He died on July 31, 1986, at the age of eighty-six.

Oskar Schindler—An Unlikely Hero

Oskar Schindler was perhaps the most colorful of the Holocaust rescuers. He was what many people would call a sharp operator. He tried many different businesses, looking for the one that would make him rich. When the Nazis came to power, he joined the party to make important contacts. When he decided to produce enamelware utensils for army field kits, he gladly used Jewish slave labor in his factory.

Schindler was on his way to making a small fortune when he began to notice the plight of his workers and the other Jews in the ghettos. He started small, making sure his people had enough to eat and were not mistreated at work. He created a haven of sorts and brought in more Jews, placing them under his protection.

A turning point came in the summer of 1942, when he witnessed Jews being packed into cattle cars and shipped to death camps. "Beyond this day, no thinking person could fail to see what would happen," he said later. "I was now resolved to do everything in my power to defeat the system."[4]

The famous "Schindler's list" of thirteen hundred names was the result. Schindler

In 1946, one year after the war ended, Oskar Schindler (second from right) posed for this picture with a small group of the many people he rescued.

named these people as "necessary workers" to save them from the deportation trains and the death camps.

By the end of the war, Oskar Schindler had made his fortune; more money than even he could have imagined. But he had spent every cent of it, keeping "his" people alive. He never did make his fortune again, or attain any position of prominence. He died penniless in 1974, at the home of friends who took care of him during his final illness. By his last request, he was buried in the Catholic cemetery on Mount Zion in Jerusalem.

Father Pierre-Marie Benoit

Father Pierre-Marie Benoit was living in the south of France when World War II began. After Germany defeated France in June 1940, the south was allowed to set up its own government under Henri Philippe Pétain. The Vichy government, as it was called, immediately started passing anti-Jewish laws.

Father Benoit was equally quick to oppose those laws. He developed a network of religious groups and anti-Nazi partisans to protect Jewish refugees.

With the help of these people, Father Benoit used every possible means to protect Jews. He found hiding places, arranged for false identity papers, and smuggled many to safety in Switzerland or Spain.

In the basement of the monastery where Father Benoit lived, a printing press churned out thousands of false baptismal certificates. With food rationing in effect, feeding all the hidden Jews was a problem. Father Benoit got ration cards from the police by pretending they were for non-Jewish refugees.

The Gestapo eventually found out about Father Benoit's activities. He fled to Rome where he continued his activities to help Jews. This humble priest worked tirelessly.

Two members of the Boogaard family in Denmark pose with two Jewish children they hid on the Pas-Op Farm. The farm was raided by the SS in October 1944. Though most of those in hiding escaped, thirty-four were captured and seven were murdered nearby.

No one knows how many lives he saved through his efforts. Father Benoit himself did not keep count.

The Danish People

Most Holocaust rescuers were individuals acting alone or in small groups. The people of Denmark were an exception. Thousands cooperated in a nationwide effort to save the country's eight thousand Jewish citizens.

From the beginning of German occupation in April 1940, the Danes refused to single out Jews. In most other ways, they cooperated with the occupational authority. They made it clear, however, that any move against the Jews would trigger widespread resistance.

The Germans had no desire to fight the Danes, whom they regarded as their racial equals. In addition, SS manpower was needed elsewhere for dealing with larger Jewish populations. The Germans did not force the issue until the war began to turn against them.

In September 1943, the Germans made plans to deport Danish Jews. On September 28, a German diplomat got word to the Danes that an "action" was scheduled for October 2.

The Danish people went to work. Jews left their homes in Copenhagen and other cities and made their way to the eastern coast.

Danish fishermen became heroes by helping transport Jewish refugees to Sweden.

There, a narrow body of water separated Denmark from neutral Sweden. The Danes hid Jews in hospitals, churches, and private homes while they carried out a huge and daring rescue operation. Using mostly small fishing boats that could only carry a few people at a time, they ferried seventy-two hundred Jews to safety. The operation took two weeks and involved at least seven hundred crossings.

Like all rescuers, the Danes were not only saving Jewish lives; they were also taking a stand against Nazism. In this sense, rescuers were like soldiers on the battlefield and partisans behind enemy lines. All were doing their part to bring down a murderous regime.

Resistance in High Places

When Adolf Hitler was striving for power, he needed the support of the German military. He got it by promising to rebuild the army and restore Germany to its rightful place of leadership in the world.

The treaty that ended World War I had crippled Germany, he said. It took away German lands, limited the military to a small force, and left the once-proud nation weak and defenseless. Now the Jews and Communism threatened Germany's very existence.

The generals listened. They were proud, aristocratic men who considered a soldier's career to be a high calling. Most of them wanted a strict government. They were used to an emperor, whose word was law. Many resented the democracy that had replaced the monarchy after World War I. Hitler knew how to speak to these concerns. He told the military leaders what they wanted to hear.

Though he was a former corporal from a lower social class, many thought he had the right idea. Many would have been horrified if they had known where that idea would lead.

The Beginnings of Military Resistance

The military leaders went along with Hitler until he had brought Germany to the brink of war. Only then did some of them think of resistance. As career officers schooled in military operations, they knew that Germany was not ready to fight another war. It lacked weapons and materials.

Unfortunately, they could not convince Hitler of this. When he ordered the invasion of Poland, they predicted that it would lead to all-out war—and disaster for Germany. Hitler predicted only victory. His blitzkrieg, or "lightning war," would win the day, he said.

The idea was to strike hard and fast with overwhelming force. Victory would come so quickly that the lack of long-term resources would not matter.

It would not be that easy, the generals warned. Britain and France had promised to defend Poland. They would declare war on Germany and all of Europe would soon become a battleground.

On the day before German troops invaded Poland, Admiral Wilhelm Canaris told a friend, "This is the end of Germany."[1]

Canaris and others considered trying to overthrow Hitler while there still might be time to stop a disaster. They never got the

Many German generals were nervous over the prospect of invading Poland. The sign reading "Zur Front" is meant to direct the German soldiers to the front in Poland where the fighting was taking place.

chance. The blitzkrieg worked, just as Hitler had said it would. Germany crushed Poland in only twenty-six days.

Britain and France declared war, but they did not mount an immediate attack on Germany. The German army marched through Western Europe, conquering one nation after another. On June 14, 1940, German troops took Paris, knocking France out of the war.

Britain stood alone against an enemy that suddenly seemed unbeatable. In Germany, everyone hailed the Führer as a military genius. Any form of open resistance would have been useless. For the time being at least, Hitler could not be toppled.

The resistance movement fell apart. It would not come together again until the fortunes of war turned against Germany.

Moral Resistance

There were those in the German ruling class who despised Nazi racism and brutality. It went against everything they believed about decent and honorable behavior. Unfortunately, most of them felt helpless to do anything about it.

They had no control over ghettos and death camps. Nothing they could say or do would change Hitler's mind about Jews and other people who were considered subhuman. They knew this and it became an excuse for looking away.

Count Helmuth von Moltke could not look away. He opposed Nazism at every opportunity and sought ways to help its victims. Even before the Nazis set up ghettos and death camps, he foresaw a terrible fate for Germany's Jews. He personally helped many to get out of the country.

A member of the ruling class, Count Helmuth von Moltke was witness to many executions. Here, a Jew lies dead after being shot by Germans retreating through Poland.

Later, when his fears had become reality, he watched the deportations and murders with growing horror. "May I know this and yet sit at my table in my heated flat and have tea? Don't I thereby become guilty too? What shall I say when I am asked: and what did you do during that time?"[2]

Von Moltke was an attorney by profession. He was also a scholar and a thinker. His way of opposing Nazism was to form what came to be known as the Kreisau circle. The name came from Von Moltke's country estate in Silesia.

A group of friends gathered there in secrecy to plan resistance activities. They came from many different walks of life and political opinions. They shared a desire to bring down Adolf Hitler and restore the rule of law in Germany.

Reversals of Fortune

So long as Germany seemed to be winning the war, neither the Kreisau circle nor the military would dare attack Hitler. Even criticizing him in public was dangerous. The German people and most of the leadership still revered him. The resistance could only watch and wait for an opportunity to act.

The long fall began after Germany invaded the Soviet Union in June 1941. Hitler had promised to destroy Communism before it destroyed Germany. He planned to hit hard and fast with overwhelming force, blitzkrieg-style. He promised that German troops would be home before winter.

It did not work out that way. The Russians fought fiercely in defense of their homeland. Instead of coming home victorious, the German army got trapped by the deadly Russian winter. Temperatures were well below zero. Vehicles would not run. Weapons would not fire.

The German throws a grenade at Russian defenders. The Russian front proved deadly for many German soldiers. As the casualty reports came in, some German officers began to turn against Hitler.

The Russian front became a nightmare for Germany. The fighting dragged into yet another winter. Hitler blamed his generals for the difficulties and would not listen to their advice.

When they wanted to move the army back to positions that could be more easily defended, he refused. There would be no retreat, he said, and no surrender. He would continue believing this until the bitter end.

While German troops slogged through impossible conditions in Russia, the German homeland came under attack from the air. British and American bombers flew regular missions over Germany, bombing cities as well as war plants and military installations.

The German people lived under siege. They worried for loved ones on the Russian front and for themselves at home in their beds. The war had become a nightmare and there was no relief in sight.

The Road From Stalingrad

After Germany's defeat at Stalingrad in early 1943, even many Nazi loyalists realized that the war was all but lost. Adolf Hitler refused to accept that. Germany could yet triumph, he claimed. Anyone who said otherwise was guilty of treason. He blamed his generals for Stalingrad and turned on them at every

Field Marshal Wilhelm Keitel remained faithful to Hitler until the end. Here, Keitel is shown signing surrender terms at the Russian headquarters in Berlin, Germany, on May 7, 1945. He was later arrested and tried in Nuremberg for war crimes. He was found guilty and executed on October 16, 1946.

opportunity. He had always been subject to towering rages. Now they were longer and louder.

Public morale plunged along with Germany's fortunes in war. However, Hitler refused to deal with that, or even acknowledge it. General Georg Thomas became concerned about the morale of the people. He suggested to Field Marshal Wilhelm Keitel that Hitler should be told of the mood in the nation. Keitel's reply was harsh. "The Führer is not interested in such [things]. It is his conviction that if the German people do not want to understand him and fight, they will have to perish."[3]

Hitler himself said the same thing, many times. He made it clear that if his empire went down, he would take the German nation—and the German people—with it.

The Plot to Kill Hitler

By the summer of 1944, it was clear to most within the resistance that Hitler was losing his grip. It was also clear that Germany was losing the war. The only hope for salvaging something was to sue for peace immediately. That would be impossible so long as Adolf Hitler was in power.

The resistance had neither the resources nor the time to mount a revolution and overthrow the Nazis. They decided that the only thing to do was assassinate Adolf Hitler.

Colonel Claus von Stauffenberg was chosen for the mission, since he attended staff meetings with the Führer. On July 7 and again on July 15, he took explosives to those meetings, but never got the chance to plant them.

Some high-ranking German officers blamed Hitler for the destruction of Germany and its army's heavy losses on the battlefield. Here, Hitler views bomb damage to a German city in 1944.

Finally, on July 20, he carried a bomb in a briefcase. He set the case under the table next to Hitler and then left the room to take a phone call. Moments later, the bomb exploded.

By chance, the briefcase had been shoved aside by someone's foot. A thick stone table leg had sheltered Hitler from the blast. He was not even seriously wounded.

The attempt to rid Germany of Hitler had failed. In Berlin, Munich, and other cities, conspirators paid the price of failure. Most of them were executed after unfair trials. The war went on, bloody and more pointless by the day. The Final Solution went on too as the Nazis scurried to finish what they had started before they ran out of time. The skies around the death camps filled with human ashes.

Hitler survived for ten more months and in that time thousands died every day. "We'll not [surrender]," Hitler said. "Never. We can go down, but we'll take a world with us."[4]

On April 30, 1945, Adolf Hitler took his own life while his empire crumbled around him. Germany surrendered a week later. The war in Europe was over.

Only later would historians evaluate the efforts at resistance, revolt, and rescue. On the surface, it was not an impressive record. Resistance movements and revolts never

Pictured in this May 19, 1947, photo are survivors of the destruction of the Jewish community of Chelm, Poland. In the five years that the Germans occupied Chelm, most of the Jewish people were sent to death camps and all of the Jewish buildings were destroyed.

came close to toppling the Nazi regime. Rescue only saved lives by the thousands while people were dying by the millions.

However, numbers do not tell the whole story. Every rescue was a life saved that otherwise would have been lost. Every act of defiance was a blow for human decency in a world gone mad and murderous.

Timeline

January 30, 1933—Hitler sworn in as chancellor of Germany.

February 28, 1933—Presidential decree grants Hitler emergency powers.

March 5, 1933—Reichstag elections. Nazis and their Nationalist allies win a slim majority.

March 24, 1933—Reichstag passes Enabling Law, giving Hitler dictatorial powers.

September 1, 1939—Germany invades Poland. World War II begins.

April 1940—Denmark occupied by German troops.

June 1940—Germany defeats France and sends an occupation force into the northern part of the country.

July 1940—Polish Jewish refugees in Lithuania ask Chiune Sugihara for help.

July 31–August 28, 1940—Chiune Sugihara hands out thousands of immigrant visas to endangered Jews.

June 22, 1941—Germany invades Soviet Union.

July 6, 1942—Anne Frank and her family go into hiding in Amsterdam.

January 18, 1943—Germans begin mass deportations from the Warsaw ghetto.

February 2, 1943—German Army defeated at Stalingrad.

February 18, 1943—Hans and Sophie Scholl arrested while passing out anti-Nazi leaflets.

April 19, 1943—Germans begin destruction of the ghetto.

June 1943—Heinrich Himmler orders all ghettos in Poland and Soviet Union destroyed.

July 25, 1943—Benito Mussolini removed from power in Italy.

August 2, 1943—Prisoner revolt at the Treblinka death camp.

September 1943—The Germans make plans to deport Danish Jews.

September 28, 1943—The Danes get word of German plans for deportation. A massive rescue operation begins.

October 1, 1943—Germans try to deport Danish Jews, triggering a giant rescue effort on the part of the Danes.

October 14, 1943—Prisoner revolt at the Sobibor death camp.

March 13, 1944—Hannah Szenes and other young Jews parachute into Yugoslavia.

April 16, 1944—Roundups of Hungarian Jews begin.

June 8, 1944—Hannah Szenes arrested by German troops.

July 20, 1944—Attempt to assassinate Adolf Hitler fails.

August 1944—Anne Frank and family discovered and arrested.

November 7, 1944—Hannah Szenes executed by firing squad.

March 1945—Anne Frank dies at the Bergen-Belsen concentration camp.

April 15, 1945—Bergen-Belsen liberated by Russian army.

April 30, 1945—Adolf Hitler commits suicide.

May 7, 1945—Germany surrenders to Allies. The war in Europe ends.

Chapter Notes

Chapter 1. Taking a Stand

1. Henry Ashby Turner, Jr., *Hitler's Thirty Days to Power* (Reading, Mass.: Addison Wesley Publishing Co., 1995), p. 147.

2. Ian Kershaw, *Hitler: 1889–1936: Hubris* (New York: W.W. Norton, 1998), p. 458.

3. Ibid., p. 464.

4. George L. Mosse, *Nazi Culture* (New York: Schocken Books, Inc., 1981), p. 278.

5. Ilse-Margret Vogel, *Bad Times, Good Friends* (New York: Harcourt Brace Jovanovich, Publishers, 1992), p. ix.

6. Jewish Virtual Library, "Martin Niemoeller," *The American-Israeli Cooperative Enterprise*, 2001, <http://www.us-israel.org/jsource/biography/niemoeller.html> (November 29, 2001).

7. Jacob G. Hornberger, "The White Rose: A Lesson in Dissent," *The American-Israeli Cooperative Enterprise*, 2001, <http://www.us-iisrael.org/jsource/Holocaust/rose.html> (December 11, 2001).

8. Inge Scholl, *The White Rose* (Hanover, N.H.: Wesleyan University Press, 1983), p. 11.

Chapter 2. The Resistance Fighters

1. Adolf Hitler, trans. Ralph Manheim, *Mein Kampf* (Boston, Mass.: Houghton Mifflin Co., 1971), p. 231.

2. Rich Cohen, *The Avengers: A Jewish War Story* (New York: Alfred A. Knopf, 2000), p. 85.

3. Ibid., p. 47.

4. Israel Gutman, *Resistance: The Warsaw Ghetto Uprising* (New York: Houghton Mifflin Co., 1994), p. 176.

5. "The Stroop Report on the Warsaw Ghetto Uprising," Quoted in *A Teacher's Guide to the Holocaust*, <http://fcit.coedu.usf.edu/holocaust/resource/document/DocStroo.htm> (December 12, 2001).

6. Ibid.

7. Vladka Meed, *On Both Sides of the Wall: Memoirs From the Warsaw Ghetto* (Washington, D.C.: United States Holocaust Memorial Museum,1993), p. 145.

8. Ibid.

Chapter 3. An Uncertain Freedom

1. United States Holocaust Memorial Museum, *Historical Atlas of the Holocaust* (New York: Macmillan Publishing, 1996), p. 198.

2. Ibid., p. 546.

3. Alicia Appleman-Jurman, *Alicia: My Story* (New York: Bantam Books, 1988), p. 139.

4. Renee Roth-Hanno, "A Girlhood in Occupied France: A Dual Experience," *Anti-Defamation League* <http://www.adl.org/hidden/between_religions/hc_7-1-girlhood_in_occupied_france.html> (December 28, 2001).

Chapter 4. To Save a People

1. Miep Gies, *Anne Frank Remembered: The Story of the Woman Who Helped to Hide the Frank Family* (New York: Simon and Schuster, 1988), p. 11.

2. Alan Levy, *The Wiesenthal File* (Grand Rapids, Mich.: William B. Eerdmans Publishing Co., 1993), p. 145.

3. Ron Greene, "Visas for Life: The Remarkable Story of Chiune and Yukiko Sugihara," *Sugihara Family Trust*, 1995–1997, <http://www.us-israel.org/jsource/Holocaust/sugihara.html> (November 29, 2001).

4. Jewish Virtual Library, "Oskar Schindler," *The American-Israeli Cooperative Enterprise*, 2001, <http://www.us-israel.org/jsource/biography/schindler.html> (December 31, 2001).

Chapter 5. Resistance in High Places

1. Theodore S. Hamerow, *On the Road to the Wolf's Lair: German Resistance to Hitler*

(Cambridge, Mass.: The Belknap Press of Harvard University Press, 1997), p. 213.

2. Michael Burleigh, *The Third Reich: A New History* (New York: Hill and Wang, 2000), p. 694.

3. Allen Welsh Dulles, *Germany's Underground: The Anti-Nazi Resistance* (New York: Da Capo Press, 2000), p. 65.

4. Ian Kershaw, *Hitler: 1889–1936: Hubris* (New York: W.W. Norton, 1998), p. 685.

Glossary

anti-Semitism—Hatred of, or discrimination against, Jews as a group.

Aryan—Nazi term for Nordic, or Northern European, peoples.

chancellor—Head of state in a parliamentary government.

civil rights—The rights of people to political and social freedom and equality.

communism—A form of government in which property is communally owned and government controlled.

concentration camp—Prison camp where people thought to be enemies of the Nazis were held for prolonged periods. Marked by brutal treatment and the use of prisoners as slave laborers.

decree—A formal and authoritative order.

Final Solution—The term applied to Nazi plans to exterminate the Jewish people.

Gestapo (Geheime-Staats-Polizei)—A secret state police agency in Nazi Germany.

Holocaust—Originally, an all-consuming fire. Used to describe the extermination of more than eleven million people, including six million Jews.

master race—Nazi term for Germanic peoples who were regarded as superior to all other "races."

monastery—A residence for monks; men who have taken religious vows.

Nazi party—National Socialist German Workers Party. The party of Adolf Hitler.

partisan—A small band of guerilla fighters operating behind enemy lines.

police state—A government in which the will of a dictatorial regime is enforced by police agencies possessing broad powers.

propaganda—A presentation of ideas slanted to shape and control public opinion.

racism—An irrational belief in the superiority of a given group, based upon inborn "racial" traits.

rationing—Limiting allowances of food and other necessities in times of scarcity.

Reichstag—The German parliament, or legislative body.

scourge—An instrument of punishment.

socialism—Public ownership or control of the means of production, distribution and exchange. The goal is to operate for use rather than for profit.

SS (Shutzstaffel)—"protection squad"; the elite guard of the Nazi state. It administered the Final Solution and insured obedience to the dictates of the Führer.

stereotype—A set of characteristics believed to be possessed by all members of a particular group.

trade union—An organization of workers in a particular occupation or industry with the goal of securing better wages, benefits, and working conditions for all its members.

Further Reading

Ayer, Eleanor H., Helen Waterford, and Alfons Heck. *Parallel Journeys*. New York: Aladdin Paperbacks, 2000.

Dvorson, Alexa. *Hitler Youth: Marching Toward Madness*. New York: Rosen Publishing Group, 1998.

Glick, Susan. *Heroes of the Holocaust*. Farmington Hills, Minn.: Gale Group, 2002.

Levine, Ellen. *Darkness over Denmark: The Danish Resistance and the Rescue of the Jews*. New York: Holiday House, Inc., 2002.

Opdyke, Irene Gut, and Jenifer Armstrong. *In My Hands: Memories of a Holocaust Rescuer*. New York: Random House Audio Publishing Group, 2002.

Rogasky, Barbara. *Smoke and Ashes: The Story of the Holocaust*. New York: Holiday House, Inc., 2002.

Sheehan, Sean. *Survival and Resistance*. Chicago, Ill.: Raintree Publishers, 2002.

Thompson, Bruce, ed. *Oskar Schindler*. Farmington Hills, Minn.: Gale Group, 2002.

Internet Addresses

The Holocaust History Project
http://www.holocaust-history.org/

Simon Wiesenthal Center: Multimedia Learning Center
http://motlc.wiesenthal.org/index.html

United States Holocaust Memorial Museum
http://www.ushmm.org

Index